Contents

Introducing eagles

There are many different types of eagle in the world. These amazing **birds of prey** are skilled and deadly hunters. But they are also beautiful creatures, soaring far above the ground.

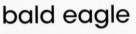

bald eagle

Charlotte Guillain

» Walk on the Wild Side «

Raintree

Raintree is an imprint of Capstone Global Library Limited, a company incorporated in England and Wales having its registered office at 7 Pilgrim Street, London, EC4V 6LB – Registered company number: 6695582

www.raintreepublishers.co.uk
myorders@raintreepublishers.co.uk

Edited by Daniel Nunn, Rebecca Rissman, and Catherine Veitch
Designed by Victoria Allen
Picture research by Mica Brancic
Production by Victoria Fitzgerald
Originated by Capstone Global Library Ltd
Printed and bound in China by CTPS

ISBN 978 1 406 26082 3 (hardback)
17 16 15 14 13
10 9 8 7 6 5 4 3 2 1

ISBN 978 1 406 26089 2 (paperback)
18 17 16 15 14
10 9 8 7 6 5 4 3 2 1

British Library Cataloguing in Publication Data
Guillain, Charlotte.
Soaring eagles. -- (Walk on the wild side)
598.9'42-dc23
A full catalogue record for this book is available from the British Library.

Acknowledgements
We would like to thank the following for permission to reproduce photographs: Corbis pp. 14 (Reuters/Shamil Zhumatov); FLPA pp. 21 (David Tipling), 23 (Harri Taavetti), 27 (Michael Callan); Getty Images pp. 9 (Oxford Scientific/Gavin Parsons), 17 (National Geographic/Klaus Nigge); Nature Picture Library pp. 4 (© Matthew Maran), 5 (© Edwin Giesbers), 7 (© Roy Mangersnes), 10 (© Pete Cairns), 11 (© Hanne & Jens Eriksen), 13© David Tipling, 15 (© Roy Mangersnes), 16 (© Tony Heald), 18 (© Pete Cairns), 20 (© Angelo Gandolfi), 24 (© Grzegorz Lesniewski), 25 (© Louis Gagnon), 26 (© Wild Wonders of Europe/Shpilenok), 28 (© Luis Quinta), 29 (© Markus Varesvuo); Photoshot p. 22 (© NHPA/Jaanus Jarva); Shutterstock pp. 8 (janbugno), 12 (© Paul van den Berg), 19 (© Rihardzz).

Cover photograph of an American Bald Eagle reproduced with permission of Getty Images (Rolf Hicker).

We would like to thank Michael Bright for his invaluable help in the preparation of this book.

Every effort has been made to contact copyright holders of material reproduced in this book. Any omissions will be rectified in subsequent printings if notice is given to the publisher.

All the Internet addresses (URLs) given in this book were valid at the time of going to press. However, due to the dynamic nature of the Internet, some addresses may have changed, or sites may have changed or ceased to exist since publication. While the author and publisher regret any inconvenience this may cause readers, no responsibility for any such changes can be accepted by either the author or the publisher.

Some words are shown in bold, **like this**. You can find out what they mean by looking in the glossary.

Harpy eagles are one of the largest eagles in the world.

harpy eagle

Where do eagles live?

Eagles live all over the world except in the **continent** of Antarctica. They live wherever there are high places for them to build their nests and **prey** for them to hunt.

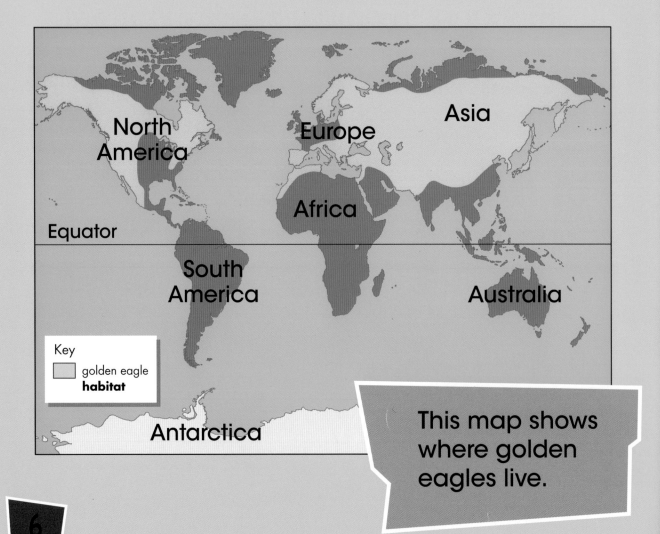

North America

Europe

Asia

Africa

Equator

South America

Australia

Key

golden eagle **habitat**

Antarctica

This map shows where golden eagles live.

Most golden
eagles live in
California, USA.

What do eagles look like?

All eagles have feathers on their heads and bodies. Bald eagles are not bald at all. They have white feathers on their heads.

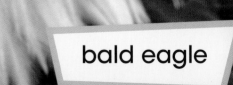

bald eagle

Many eagles have a **crest** on their heads.

hawk eagle

Wings and tails

All eagles have long, wide wings and a large fan-shaped tail. Their wings allow them to **glide** for long distances. Eagles can bend the tips of their wings to help them steer. They also move their tails to change direction and fly higher or lower.

golden eagle

Eagles' long wing feathers are stiff and shaped so the air moves over the wing smoothly.

Bonelli's eagle

Beaks and talons

Eagles have very large, strong beaks. They are hooked and sharp, so they are a perfect tool for ripping **prey** to pieces. Eagles also have sharp, curved **talons**.

golden eagle

beak

Harpy eagles have huge talons. They use them to catch larger prey, such as monkeys.

talon

Hunting

Different types of eagle hunt different **prey**. Many eagles, such as golden eagles and wedge-tailed eagles, **glide** high above ground looking for birds and small **mammals**.

Golden eagles mainly hunt rabbits, hares, and other small mammals.

Sea eagles fly over water and snatch up fish in their **talons**.

Different skills

Eagles hunt in different ways. Golden eagles **glide** over open ground before diving down to catch **prey**. Philippine eagles snatch up prey such as monkeys from the branches in forests.

Serpent eagles hunt on the forest floor where they stab prey with their **talons**.

Philippine eagle

xcellent ey sight

Eagles' large eyes can see **prey** below them from as far as a kilometre away. Eagles have two types of vision. They can see in front of them, the way humans do. They can also see out to the sides.

golden eagle

Did you know?

Unlike many animals, eagles can see in colour.

bald eagle

Diving

When a golden eagle spots **prey**, it starts to dive to the ground very quickly. It can dive at 240 kilometres per hour. Eagles often tuck in their wings when they dive, to make them more **streamlined**.

Did you know?

Golden eagles often hunt in pairs, with one chasing prey and the other swooping in to kill.

Partners

Golden eagles live in pairs, with one male and one female eagle. They stay together for many years, sometimes all their lives. Each pair of golden eagles has its own **territory**. This is an area of land that provides the food they need.

Did you know?

A golden eagle's territory can be as big as 155 square kilometres.

female

male

23

Eyries

Pairs of golden eagles make their huge nests together in very high places. An eagle's nest is called an eyrie. Eagles build their eyries out of sticks and leaves. They often use the same nest for several years.

Golden eagles build nests in trees, on cliffs, or even on telegraph poles.

bald eagle eyrie

Fyggs and eaglets

Eagles lay between one and four eggs. The parents share the job of sitting on the eggs and keeping them warm. Baby eagles are called eaglets. They are covered in soft **down** when they hatch.

golden eagle

The parents sit on their eggs for around 45 days.

Eaglets are fed by their parents until they are old enough to hunt.

golden eagle

Life for an eagle

Eagles are among the most majestic birds in the sky. It is important that humans protect these beautiful birds and their **habitats**, so they don't die out.

golden eagle

Did you know?

Eagles can live for up to 30 years.

golden eagle

Glossary

bird of prey bird that hunts and kills birds and other animals for food

continent large land mass, such as Asia, Europe, or Antarctica

crest feathers sticking up on a bird's head

down first, soft feathers on a baby bird

glide move smoothly

habitat natural home for an animal or plant

mammal hair-covered animal that feeds its young on milk

prey animal hunted by another animal for food

streamlined shaped to move easily through air or water

talon bird of prey's claw

territory area of land where one animal or group of animals lives

Find out more

Books

Birds of Prey, Peter Holden (Usborne, 2006)

Eagles, Sally Morgan (Franklin Watts, 2010)

Exploring the World of Eagles, Tracy C. Read (Firefly Books, 2010)

Websites

kids.nationalgeographic.com/kids/animals/creaturefeature/baldeagle/
The National Geographic website has information on many animals, including bald eagles.

www.bbc.co.uk/nature/life/Golden_Eagle
Watch videos of golden eagles on the BBC Nature website.

www.globio.org/glossopedia/article.aspx?art_id=48&art_nm=Eagles
Find out more about eagles on the Globio website.

Index